Pirates and Privateers
in the New World
MOMENTS IN HISTORY

SHIRLEY JORDAN

Perfection Learning®

About the Author

Shirley Jordan is a retired elementary school teacher and principal. Currently a lecturer in the teacher-training program at California State University, Fullerton, California, she sees exciting things happening in the world of social studies. Shirley loves to travel—with a preference for sites important to U.S. history.

Shirley has had more than 50 travel articles published in recent years. It was through her travels that she became interested in "moments in history," those ironic and little-known stories that make one exclaim, "I didn't know that!" Such stories are woven throughout her books.

Image Credits: CORBIS/Bettmann pp. 28 (bottom), 59; © NATIONAL MARITIME MUSEUM PICTURE LIBRARY, LONDON pp. 14, 16 (top), 19, 41, 46; New York Public Library, Tilden Foundation p. 54

Images for timeline are all ArtToday except Library of Congress p. 4 (top) and Photo Disc p. 4 (bottom right); ArtToday (www.arttoday.com) pp. 3, 7, 8, 10, 11 (top), 11 (middle), 12, 13 (bottom), 15, 16 (bottom), 17, 18, 20 (top), 21, 22, 23, 24, 25, 26, 27, 28 (top), 29, 34 (top), 36, 37, 39, 40, 42 (bottom), 44, 47, 52, 58, 60, 61, 62, 64, 65, 66, 72; Corel pp. 6, 56; Shirley Jordan pp. 32, 33; Library of Congress pp. 4 (top), 11 (bottom right), 11 (bottom left), 13 (top), 20 (bottom), 30, 34 (bottom), 42 (top), 43, 45, 48, 49, 50, 51, 53, 55, 57, 63; PhotoDisc pp. 4 (bottom right), 9, 31, 35, 38

Text © 2001 by **Perfection Learning® Corporation**.
All rights reserved. No part of this book may be used or reproduced in any manner whatsoever without written permission from the publisher.
Printed in the United States of America. For information, contact Perfection Learning® Corporation, 1000 North Second Avenue, P.O. Box 500, Logan, Iowa 51546-0500.
Tel: 1-800-831-4190 • Fax: 1-712-644-2392
Paperback ISBN 0-7891-5396-3
Cover Craft® ISBN 0-7807-9803-1

4 5 6 PP 06

Table of Contents

Timeline of Important Events 4
Chapter 1   Attack on the High Seas 6
Chapter 2   Pirates of the New World 10
Chapter 3   The Beginning of Piracy in the Americas 12
Chapter 4   The Treasure Galleons of the Spanish Main 15
Chapter 5   Life on Board the Pirate Ship 19
Chapter 6   The Pirate Code of Conduct 21
Chapter 7   A Queen's Privateers 23
Chapter 8   L'Olonnois the Cruel 27
Chapter 9   Morgan the Terrible 32
Chapter 10   A Musical Pirate 37
Chapter 11   Captain William Kidd 39
Chapter 12   Blackbeard the Pirate 44
Chapter 13   Stede Bonnet, a Gentleman Pirate 49
Chapter 14   Black Bart the Pirate 50
Chapter 15   Two Women Under the Jolly Roger Flag 52
Chapter 16   Low and Phillips 57
Chapter 17   Privateers and the American Revolution 58
Chapter 18   Jean Lafitte 59
Chapter 19   California's Pirate 63
Chapter 20   Piracy Comes to an End in the New World 67
     Glossary 68
     Index 71

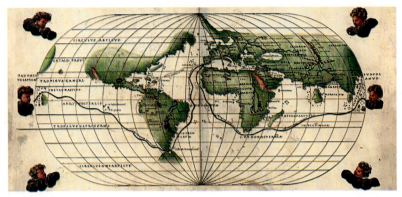

Timeline of Important Events

1562 Francis Drake becomes captain of his own ship. He begins raids upon Spanish ships.

The **pirate** John Hawkins becomes a slave trader.

1572 Drake attacks Nombre de Dios, Panama.

1577 Drake sets out on a three-year trip around the world.

1588 Both Drake and Hawkins fight for England against the **Spanish Armada**.

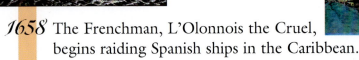

1658 The Frenchman, L'Olonnois the Cruel, begins raiding Spanish ships in the Caribbean.

1668 Henry Morgan is **commissioned** as a **privateer** for the English **Crown**. He becomes famous all over the Caribbean.

1689 Gustav Wilmerding becomes captain of his own ship. Music is important to this Caribbean pirate.

1695 Captain Kidd receives a privateer's commission from England's Lord Bellomont. Later, Kidd is hanged for his crimes.

1716 The pirate Blackbeard takes over the waters off the Carolinas and Virginia.

1718 Blackbeard **blockades** the harbor at Charleston, South Carolina, for nearly two weeks.

The pirate Stede Bonnet is hanged in Charleston.

1719 Black Bart becomes a pirate captain.

1720 Calico Jack Rackham is hanged. Anne Bonny and Mary Read escape **execution**.

1723 The pirate Edward Low is captured off Long Island.

1724 John Phillips is murdered by his crew. His head is returned to Boston.

1776 Privateers and their ships begin helping the colonists in their fight against the British navy during the years of the American Revolution.

1807 Jean Lafitte, slaver and pirate, takes control of the waters around New Orleans.

1814–1815 Lafitte helps save New Orleans from British attack at the close of the War of 1812.

1818 Hippolyte de Bouchard raids and burns Monterey, the capital of California.

CHAPTER 1

Attack on the High Seas

PICTURE a blue-green, sparkling sea. Imagine that you are a well-to-do Spanish merchant. You're sailing aboard a fine treasure **galleon**. Such a fine ship has a strong wooden **hull** and three tall, powerful **masts**.

Above your head billow vast clouds of canvas. Gusts of wind howl through the *rigging*. This web of thick ropes supports the mast and controls the sails. Your vessel carries a crew of 200 men and more than 50 cannons.

But in the 1500s, things are not always peaceful on the open waters of the Atlantic Ocean.

As you look forward, dozens of other Spanish galleons stretch across the horizon. All carry riches from the New World. Gold, silver, and precious jewels have come from the mines of Peru and Mexico. Most of the treasure on this vessel belongs to you. So you have an interest in the safe journey of this group of ships, or *flota*.

Suddenly, there is a cry from the lookout high on the mast. A strange ship is approaching from behind. It comes closer and closer.

Your vessel is at the rear of the flota. It is in the greatest danger. The captain orders more crew members up from below.

Faster and faster, the unknown ship plows through the water. As it comes near, you see it is a small, **square-rigged** pirate ship. It's fast and easy to maneuver. Would these pirates dare attack a fully armed galleon?

The attackers appear to have no more than 20 cannons. But their speed gives them an advantage.

On deck, you make out the shapes of running men. They are quickly adjusting the sails for even more speed.

Will any other ships of the flota turn back to help? Two **men-of-war** are ahead of you. They are well-armed. But they are far forward. And they are guarding the largest merchant ships.

It may be that the other Spaniards have seen your **plight**. But galleons are too heavy and awkward to change direction easily. They are loaded with cargo from the mines of the Spanish colonies. If another ship dropped back to help, it would have to sail a slow, zigzag pattern into the wind. Then it would be too late for either of you to rejoin the flota.

7

No, your ship alone must defend itself.

You quickly step out of the way of crew manning the guns at the **stern**. Great blasts fill the air as cannonballs arc across the waters. The smell of gunpowder is everywhere.

But the pirate ship avoids the blasts by changing direction again and again. The shots from your galleon plunge harmlessly into the blue Caribbean waters.

Now the pirates fire back, using their **bow** cannons. Though they have smaller and older weapons, there is danger. Your galleon cannot move away quickly enough. It is now a large target. And it's within range. You stumble and fall to the deck. A cannonball hits the mast.

A battle between cannons is not what the attackers want. If they sink your ship, the treasure will be far below in the sea.

Swiftly moving into musket range, the pirates on deck raise their weapons. Carefully, they aim at the captain, the officers, and those manning your galleon's cannons. The captain and other leaders fall. A great confusion arises. Who is left to give the orders?

Before the crew around you can sort this out, the pirate ship comes alongside. You watch in terror as pirates toss ropes with hooks on the ends. These clatter to the deck.

Quickly, the attackers lash the two ships together. Dozens of pirates leap aboard. They race toward you, howling and swinging axes and swords.

A moment later, a black-toothed **ruffian** raises his dagger above your head. The sun flashes off the blade as the weapon swoops down. You slump to the deck. You're just one more victim of a pirate on the high seas.

CHAPTER 2

Pirates of the New World

WHO were these pirates? What were their roles in the history of North, Central, and South America?

Were they heroes serving their home countries? Were they explorers who saw a chance to steal from the new lands they'd discovered? Were they brave sailors who turned greedy as they became leaders?

Or were they common criminals? Were they men and women who should have been locked away in prisons?

The pirates who played a part in the history of America were a little bit of each of these things. To learn about them, we must first understand some terms.

The word *pirate* means "someone who **plunders** on the sea." Some of these fierce raiders cared only about stealing. They didn't care whose treasure they took.

Privateers were different. These were sea raiders with a license from their governments to attack enemy ships. Such a license was called a "letter of marque." Claiming the riches of the captured ship meant money for the privateer and his crew. And it meant funds for the treasury of the government that had hired them.

We sometimes hear of **buccaneers**. These were pirates of the 1600s who sailed the Caribbean Sea.

When they first arrived in the New World, buccaneers were peaceful. Most lived on the island of Hispaniola. There, they hunted wild cattle and pigs. They cooked the meat and sold it to the captains of passing ships. The name *buccaneer* comes from the word *boucan*, a type of small smokehouse for cooking meat.

Then the Spanish drove the buccaneers off their island. So, many became pirates. These rowdy raiders were famous for their cruelty and their love of **rum**.

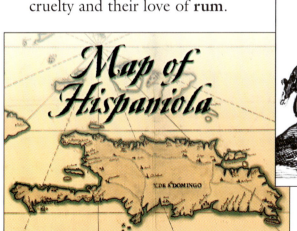

CHAPTER 3

The Beginning of Piracy in the Americas

As early as 1503, a few small Spanish settlements dotted the Americas. But they could not survive without supplies from the homeland. So trading ships traveled back and forth across the Atlantic Ocean. The Spanish king gave the harbor city of Seville, Spain, the right to run this business.

Caravel

At first, ships crossing the Atlantic were very small. Most were under 100 tons. They measured 50 to 55 feet in length. That's about as long as a large school bus. The distance across the decks was 18 feet. That's close to the width of a classroom.

These early ships were **caravels**. They were the same design as Columbus's ships, the *Niña* and the *Pinta*. With only two to four masts and **lanteen sails**, caravels sailed close to the wind and made good speed.

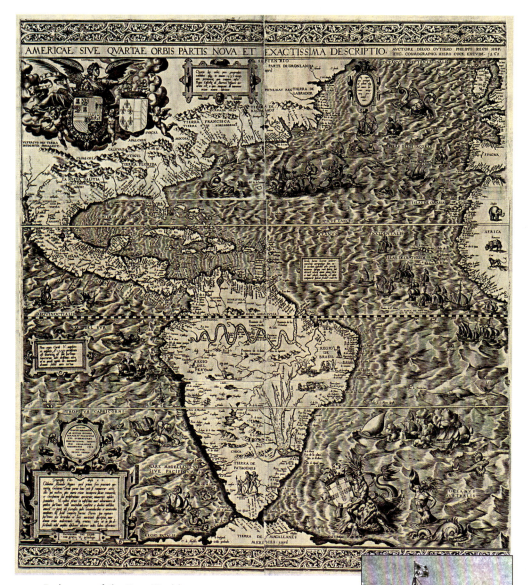

Early map of the New World

But these ships did not work well for long ocean voyages. They were too small to carry much cargo. Beginning in the 1540s, **naos**, which were larger ships, were used to deliver great quantities of goods. (Columbus's flagship, the *Santa Maria*, was a nao.)

But even naos weren't the best ships for the Spanish trade. They were large and bulky. They were shaped like bathtubs and very

Nao

slow. They did have plenty of cargo space. But faster ships could easily catch up with naos. And that was a problem.

Almost from the beginning of trade between Seville and the Spanish colonies, pirates stole whatever they could. Their targets were the caravels and naos that crossed the Atlantic Ocean.

Merchant ships carried riches no matter which direction they were headed. When they left Spain to sail to the colonies, ships carried cloth, leather goods, glassware, ironware, weapons, paper, books, musical instruments, and liquor.

Merchant ship

On return trips from the Americas, the **holds** of these ships were often filled with samples of precious metals needed to make Spanish coins. Capturing one of these ships was a pirate's dream.

The pirates were successful and happy. And each year, the riches coming from the New World increased.

In 1520, Hernando Cortés conquered the rich lands of Mexico for his homeland, Spain. And in 1533, another Spaniard, Francisco Pizarro, defeated the Incas of Peru. Now tons of gold, silver, and precious jewels were waiting to be carried to the ports of Spain.

CHAPTER 4

The Treasure Galleons of the Spanish Main

IN the late 1500s, a well-respected Spanish naval commander named Don Alvaro de Bazán began work on a design for a new ship. At first, he thought of using **galleys** for the ocean crossings.

When winds were calm, these long, low ships could be rowed by as many as 25 pairs of oarsmen. But this idea was quickly discarded. Such a ship had only one deck. Having so many men on board would require a great deal of food and water. And this would leave little space for trade goods. Besides, galleys were safe only in sheltered waters.

Bazán then designed a larger ship. It was a vessel weighing several hundred tons. It had long, straight lines and either two or three decks. It might have as many as four masts. They would all carry square sails except the **aft**, or *mizzen*, mast. That would carry a lanteen sail.

Bazán called his new design a *galleon*. These ships would be popular on the seas for more than 200 years.

In 1526, a law was passed that merchant ships sailing across the Atlantic must be properly armed. And they had to sail in groups of at least ten vessels.

The Spanish merchants liked these new rules. By 1550, a flota might contain between 50 and 100 ships.

A number of **pataches** sailed with the galleons. These smaller ships were used as messenger boats. They traveled from galleon to galleon during the long ocean voyage. Nearing land, pataches sailed to smaller, out-of-the-way settlements like St. Augustine, Florida. A sandbar there made crossing impossible for larger vessels.

Patach

The chief officers of a flota of galleons usually obtained their positions by **bribery**. These men were rich nobles or high-ranking army officers who knew little about the sea. They were on board to collect their share of the prize cargo.

Once appointed, however, they quickly hired experienced officers to run their ships. The officers, in turn, received bribes from those who would work under them. Except for navigators, who were hard to find, plenty of Spaniards applied for the jobs of officer on a galleon.

Filling the crew, however, was another matter. Spaniards had never had a tradition as **maritime** people. They left that to men from England, Norway, Holland, or Italy. Few of Spain's young men signed on to sail the galleons. So those jobs went to foreigners. It was not unusual to hear a dozen different languages on a ship's deck.

Life on board Spanish galleons was much better than some of the men had known on shore. By law, every crew member had to receive each day a quart of wine, two pounds of biscuits, one and one-half ounces of olive oil, half a quart of vinegar, and a small piece of cheese. The rules also called for eight ounces of dried fish and two ounces of peas or beans four days a week. In addition, eight ounces of salt pork and one and one-half ounces of rice were handed out three days a week.

Besides the foods called for by Spanish law, sugar, almonds, and dried fruit were stored. Pens for pigs and goats were built on the open deck or in the hold. Next to them, cages of live chickens were tied down.

Wealthy passengers often sailed on the galleons. For them, it was a pleasure cruise. Their servants sailed with them. They made sure their masters had rich and varied food from home. They brought live beasts and fowl, hams, bacon, dried fish, noodles, rice, lentils, olives, butter, spices, and dried fruit on board. Some of the richest passengers traveled with as many as 20 different kinds of wine and brandy.

Servants did the cooking on the main deck over a large metal box. Inside the box, burning wood or charcoal glowed in a nest of wet sand.

The common seamen on board had no cook assigned to them. So when the servants of the rich passengers finished with the fire, crew members lined up to use the dying coals. However, these fires were dangerous unless the sea was calm. And they were permitted only during daylight hours. So, many sailors often ate their dinners cold.

CHAPTER 5

Life on Board the Pirate Ship

THE wooden sailing ships used by the pirates were damp, dark, and filled with unpleasant odors. Lifeboats were rare. So escape during a battle or a sinking was nearly impossible.

These ships sat low in the water. In bad weather, waves washed over the decks and trickled into the holds. Clothes could stay wet for weeks.

When sailors finished their duty time on deck, they went below.

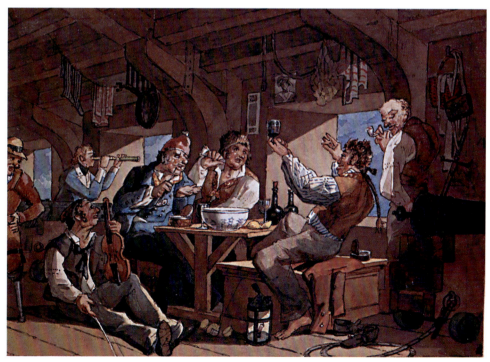

Their beds were a crowded spot in the **forecastle**, called the *fo'c's'le*, forward of the first mast. There, with just a candle for a light, they might share a soaked blanket with another crew member.

Garbage and waste collected in the damp bottom of the hull. This attracted beetles, cockroaches, and rats. It was not unusual to lose half the crew to disease during a voyage. To keep the fighting force strong, captains often carried as many as 250 men on a ship only 125 feet long.

Unlike the merchant vessels, the food carried on pirate ships was terrible. Water smelled. Meat rotted. And biscuits were dotted with black beetles. Many wise old **sea dogs** knocked their biscuits against the deck to shake out the weevils and maggots. Some chose to eat in the dark so they would not see what went into their mouths.

It was a fortunate pirate crew that found good fishing. Turtles caught in the warm Caribbean waters were special treats. In the early days of a voyage, there might be hens on board to provide eggs. But as the voyage continued, these chickens were soon eaten.

Since they followed no set schedule, pirate ships sometimes ran completely out of food. When that happened, the desperate men searched the horizon even more intently. In addition to seeking rubies, emeralds, and gold, a pirate crew might launch an attack just to capture the food stores of another ship.

On the high seas, there was more than one kind of treasure to be stolen.

CHAPTER 6

The Pirate Code of Conduct

MOST pirates had at one time been **merchant seamen**. Some were honest. Some were not. Some hated to follow orders and could be violent.

A pirate who broke the rules of the code could be **marooned** on a desert island. The captain and crew would leave the pirate with just a bottle of water and a gun. Most pirates left behind died from hunger and thirst. It was a slow, agonizing death.

But even pirates had rules. A few of the common ones included these.

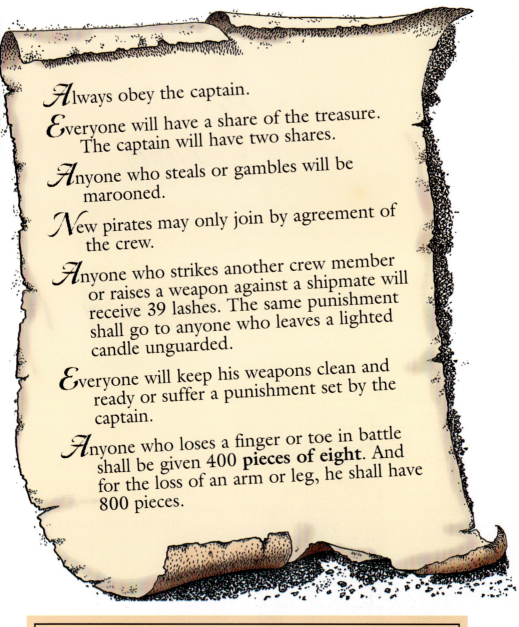

*A*lways obey the captain.

*E*veryone will have a share of the treasure. The captain will have two shares.

*A*nyone who steals or gambles will be marooned.

*N*ew pirates may only join by agreement of the crew.

*A*nyone who strikes another crew member or raises a weapon against a shipmate will receive 39 lashes. The same punishment shall go to anyone who leaves a lighted candle unguarded.

*E*veryone will keep his weapons clean and ready or suffer a punishment set by the captain.

*A*nyone who loses a finger or toe in battle shall be given 400 **pieces of eight**. And for the loss of an arm or leg, he shall have 800 pieces.

Pieces of eight were parts of Spanish coins formed from the New World's gold and silver. A Spanish *peso*, made to be cut into eight pieces, could be used for small change. Two pieces of eight would buy a cow.

CHAPTER 7

A Queen's Privateers

JOHN Hawkins and Francis Drake were English privateers. They worked for Queen Elizabeth I. The queen was happy about the many raids the men made upon Spanish merchant ships. The treasures the two captured were making her very rich. But Queen Elizabeth wanted to keep her part in the attacks a secret. England was not ready for a war with Spain.

John Hawkins

Francis Drake

Many historians believe Drake was a relative, perhaps a nephew, of John Hawkins. And it was probably through Hawkins that young Francis was given his own ship, the *Judith*, to command when he was only 22.

The Spaniards used mule trains to bring caravans of silver from the mines of Peru across the Isthmus of Panama. Drake set out to steal these vast riches. Again and again, he raided the Spaniards. His fame grew throughout the New World and Europe.

Boldly, Drake sailed the *Judith* into battle. He chased down Spanish treasure ships that were trying to sail safely from Panama to Seville, Spain. For a short time, Hawkins and Drake sailed their ships side by side. But both wanted to be the leader. The two could not work together.

Meanwhile, Hawkins turned his attention to slave trading. In 1562, he made the first of three trips from the Caribbean to Africa's coast. With him, he carried a cheap cargo of sugar and molasses.

Francis Drake

After arriving in Africa, Hawkins traded the cargo for about 300 captured African natives. He crammed them into the ship's hold and sailed back across the Atlantic.

At the island of Hispaniola, Hawkins sold his suffering captives as slaves. For the rest of their days, they would cut sugarcane in the scorching tropical heat.

In 1572, Drake left England with two ships and 73 crewmen to attack the treasure port of Nombre de Dios, Panama. This raid was so successful that the angry Spaniards named Drake "The Dragon."

The queen was pleased with both her privateers. They were her "iron men in wooden ships."

Drake's most famous voyage came in 1577. He left

Plymouth, England, with five ships including the *Golden Hind*. Drake and 164 men went in search of new lands for their queen. Sailing south to the tip of South America, he passed through the dangerous Strait of Magellan.

Drake then sailed north. He traveled up the western coast of South America, past Mexico, and on to California. There he landed. He set down a plaque to mark a bay north of what is now San Francisco. Proudly, he claimed the land for England. He named  this place New Albion. Here Drake stopped to **careen** his ship and make necessary repairs.

Drake found no riches in California. So he sailed west across the Pacific Ocean. From there, he rounded the tip of Africa, called the Cape of Good Hope.

Golden Hind

25

When he returned to England, Drake was hailed as a hero. The delighted queen rewarded him by making him a knight. From then on, he was to be called Sir Francis Drake.

Later, both Hawkins and Drake served England in the bitter 1588 battle against the Spanish Armada. By defeating the Spaniards in that battle, England became the most powerful nation on the seas.

Ferdinand Magellan, a Portuguese navigator, was first to lead a sailing expedition around the world. He died in 1531 before the journey ended. This made the English privateer, Sir Francis Drake, the first captain to circle the globe and survive.

Seamen needed to *careen* their ships when barnacles and seaweed grew too thick on the **keels**. This meant the ship was pulled up on shore, tipped to one side, then the other. Each side was burned to clear away the growth. The fire also destroyed teredo worms that could bore through the wood and cause leaks.

Teredo worm holes

Chapter 8

L'Olonnois the Cruel

JEAN-DAVID Nau had always been unlucky. He was born in 1630 in the French town of Sables l'Olonne. As a young boy, he was sold as an **indentured servant**. This means his parents gave him away for money. The new owner took the boy to the islands of the West Indies. Most islands in the West Indies were ruled by the Spanish.

France had been at war with Spain for many years. And young Nau never forgot that he was French. He came to hate everything Spanish. His anger grew stronger and stronger.

Before he had been in the Indies long, the clever young man escaped to freedom. Soon he had become captain of a French **corsair**. His ship flew two flags. One was the Jolly Roger of piracy. The other was a red flag that signaled "no **quarter** given." That meant all who resisted would be killed.

In France, men and women were often called by the town of their birth. So Jean-David Nau was known as "L'Olonnois" (LOW-len-wah.) As a pirate, he never hesitated to torture his victims. So his name soon became "L'Olonnois the Cruel." He was the bloodiest and most wicked pirate of his day.

L'Olonnois torturing his victims

L'Olonnois and his men raided Spanish ships for years, stealing cargoes and taking slaves. He could have been very rich. But few pirates ever saved their money. L'Olonnois was no different. He threw it all away in drunkenness and partying.

Before the **loot** from a captured ship was divided, there were certain debts to be paid to those pirates who had been wounded. After each battle, injuries were examined. The men under L'Olonnois's command were paid for their pain.

- For the loss of a right arm—$600 or 6 slaves
- For the loss of a left arm—$500 or 5 slaves
- For the loss of a right leg—$500 or 5 slaves
- For the loss of a left leg—$400 or 4 slaves
- For the loss of a finger or an eye—$100 or 1 slave

The rest of the stolen goods were divided. Then the share of any pirate who had died was set aside for family members.

One autumn, a huge storm wrecked L'Olonnois's ship near Campeche, Cuba. Struggling to stay afloat, the half-drowned pirates managed to get to the shore.

Suddenly, soldiers from town rushed onto the beach and attacked the pirates. With the ship in splinters, there was no escape.

L'Olonnois was afraid he would be captured. A big reward was offered to anyone hauling *him* to jail.

As the battle raged, L'Olonnois quietly dipped his hands into the bleeding wounds of the bodies on the beach. He smeared blood all over his face and neck. Then he fell to the sand, pretending to be dead.

The battle continued. He didn't move at all.

When the fighting was over, the Spaniards dragged the captured pirates into town. Thinking L'Olonnois was but one more dead pirate, they left him behind on the sand.

Singing and dancing took place in the streets. The terrible threat from the pirate L'Olonnois was over! How happy the people of Campeche were!

During the celebration, no one saw a figure sneak to the harbor, steal a boat, and sail away in the darkness.

When the governor of Cuba figured out what had happened, he sent a man-of-war after L'Olonnois. But by that time, the pirate had a new vessel and a new crew of cutthroats. He was eager for a fight.

Instead of running away, L'Olonnois got ready to trap the Spaniards. He and his men captured a large fishing boat and its crew. He forced the fishermen to sail toward the man-of-war as darkness fell.

The lookout on the huge ship called out to the smaller boat. L'Olonnois ordered one hostage fisherman to answer in Spanish. Thinking all was safe, the captain of the man-of-war sailed closer. Suddenly, the pirates jumped from the fishing boat onto the larger ship.

Most of the Spanish crew was down below. The pirates quickly captured those on deck before anyone could come up from the hold.

But L'Olonnois the Cruel was not happy simply to win the battle. He ordered the Spaniards to be brought on deck one by one. Then, waving his **cutlass**, he beheaded each of them. When he was done, 90 headless bodies were piled upon the deck.

When the last trembling man was brought up, L'Olonnois spared his life. "Tell your governor what you have seen here," he said. "This is a warning to him."

Years later, in 1667, L'Olonnois the Cruel and his men **sacked** the cities of Maracaibo and Gibraltar in Venezuela. After wasting their money on drinking and parties, the pirates attacked Puerto Cabello. But time was running out for L'Olonnois.

Near Las Perlas Island, L'Olonnois met a large Spanish fleet head on. Battling all the way, he finally reached the coast of Cartagena. There, he and some of his men escaped on land.

But freedom was not to be theirs. The pirates were caught by the fierce Carib Indians and met a terrible death. The natives, who hated whites, tore L'Olonnois apart piece by piece, burned his body, then scattered the ashes to the winds. Not even a gravestone marked the place.

Cruelty had been his way of life. And it was by cruelty that L'Olonnois died.

Chapter 9

Morgan the Terrible

Henry Morgan was an English farm boy. He had been born in Wales in 1635. As a very young man, he ran away to sea. When he arrived in the New World, he had no money. So in order to live, he sold himself to a plantation owner as an indentured servant.

At the age of 20, Morgan was desperate to get out of his indentured service. So he ran away and joined the British army. After being discharged, he joined a fellow seaman for a short time. He then took over the fleet of 15 ships they had captured.

In 1668, at age 33, Morgan was commissioned as a privateer for the English Crown. Now it was his job to raid Spanish ports and share the riches from the treasure ships with his king.

Morgan successfully attacked and looted the Cuban city of Puerto Principe. After this, he was sure he could not be stopped. Now he needed a bigger target.

Porto Bello, Panama

Morgan's men were shocked when he chose Porto Bello, Panama. Three strong forts and more than 1,000 soldiers defended the city. "We are sure to be caught," the pirates told one another. "Our captain just doesn't know how strong Porto Bello is."

The harbor was filled with Spanish galleons loaded with treasures from the mines of Panama and Chile. And to protect them, the city's guns were pointed toward the sea. Morgan and his nine ships would have to pass that point.

But Henry Morgan had a special plan. He loaded his best fighting men into stolen fishing canoes. After dark, they silently slid into the harbor.

Porto Bello, Panama

His trick worked. The Spanish guns were of no use. They were aimed too high. Two of the forts were easily overcome by the pirates.

At the third fort, the pirates tried to scale the wall. Spanish soldiers threw rocks and poured hot oil down on them. Morgan saw that there was no way to mount the

Porto Bello, Panama

Henry Morgan

walls. So he ordered his men to build long, wide ladders. Then he forced some captured nuns and monks to go up the ladders first. The pirates followed.

The governor of Porto Bello refused to give up his fort. He ordered his men to fire upon anyone on the ladders.

Many of the nuns and monks were killed. They fell from the ladders. But they had shielded the pirates below them. The pirates soon scaled the walls. With yells of victory, the attackers killed almost every Spaniard. They captured 250,000 pieces of eight and 300 slaves.

Now Morgan had earned the nickname "Morgan the Terrible." He became so famous that evil pirates from all over the Caribbean Sea wanted to join up with him. Soon he had 15 ships and 900 men.

Between raids, the pirates needed somewhere to repair and careen their ships. The colony of Jamaica became that place. Governor Modyford of Jamaica liked Morgan because he brought many Spanish goods to the island. Often Morgan gave the dishonest governor some of his riches.

Again, Morgan became restless. Needing a new target, he sailed to Venezuela. Two wealthy cities waited there, Maracaibo and Gibraltar. They were located at opposite ends of a large inland body of water, Lake Maracaibo.

Word had spread about the arrival of Henry Morgan. The people of the two cities gathered their riches and ran into the hills. When Morgan arrived, he found both places almost deserted. He ordered his men to find the Spaniards who had run away.

For eight weeks, the pirates searched. Each week, they found some of those in hiding and dragged them into town. There the captives from Maracaibo and Gibraltar were tortured until they told where their money was hidden.

When it seemed he had captured all the riches of the two cities, Morgan wanted to return to Jamaica. But as he tried to sail out of Lake Maracaibo, he found three huge Spanish warships blocking his path to the open sea. The strong fort at the entrance to the sea had its cannons aimed directly at him. For the first time in his life, Morgan was trapped.

Morgan thought. He paced his deck. Then he came up with a plan. He ordered his men to load the hold of a ship they had captured with gunpowder, tar, and pitch. Then he had the men make dummies. They used logs for bodies and pumpkins for heads.

The dummies were dressed in pirate clothes. Then they were arranged on the deck of the fire ship.

Morgan sent a message to the Spaniards. He told the admiral of the largest ship that he would burn the town of Gibraltar unless he was allowed to sail out to sea.

But the admiral would not allow the pirates to pass.

At dawn the next day, the pirate's ships moved forward. The fire ship was in the lead. It headed for the largest Spanish ship, the *Magdalena*.

With cannons firing at them from the shore, Morgan's sailors brought the fire ship up against the *Magdalena*. They tied the two vessels together. Then they threw lighted matches into the hold of the fire ship and jumped overboard.

The fire ship blew up in a single great cloud of flames and smoke. Wood flew everywhere.

The sails on the *Magdalena* caught fire. Her decks were soon ablaze. As the fire reached her supply of gunpowder, there was another horrible explosion.

The two ships sank under the water. Most of the Spanish sailors were drowned. Of the other two warships, one burned and sank. The other was easily taken by the pirates.

Now the only thing in Morgan's way was the fort with its cannons pointed his way. Again, the crafty Morgan turned to trickery. He ordered his men into a longboat. "Row into a sheltered cove downstream from the fort," he told them. "Then lie down on the bottom of the boat and have the oarsman row you back."

The boat made its trips back and forth to shore. Spanish soldiers in the fort were fooled into thinking that Morgan's men were landing a large force on shore.

The soldiers were sure the pirates were planning to attack the fort from the land. So before night fell, the officers ordered the soldiers to turn their cannons around to face the jungle.

As the moon came up, Morgan's ships sailed silently down the waters of the channel. They had entered the Caribbean before the soldiers in the fort knew they'd been fooled.

In 1671, Morgan and his men attacked Panama City. The Spaniards defending the city let loose a herd of bulls. But the bulls stampeded. Instead of attacking the pirates, the angry animals turned on the Spanish soldiers. Morgan was able to take most of the city's treasures.

But this pirate attack violated a peace agreement signed between Spain and England the year before. Morgan was arrested and brought before his king, Charles II.

When the king later forgave him, Morgan moved back to Jamaica. There he lived peacefully until his death in 1688.

Charles II

CHAPTER 10

A Musical Pirate

IN addition to the captain, quartermaster, officers, and ordinary seamen, others sailed with the pirate crews of the Caribbean. Most ships carried an orchestra of sorts. Many of the musicians were seamen who had been captured from other ships and pressed into service. A man who could play an instrument was always a welcome prize.

While in port, the musicians were on call to play **jigs** or **hornpipes** at pirate dances. Often they played for their fellow pirates during dinner.

But their most important duty came during battle. They played nautical tunes, **sea chanteys**, or fight songs on drums, trumpets, and bugles. The music encouraged their own men and frightened their enemies.

The pirate captain proudest of his band was a Dane named Gustav Wilmerding. His pirate kingdom was in a cove called Soper's Hole on the island of Tortola.

Wilmerding had first gone to sea in 1682. He had left Denmark as a cabin boy on a merchant ship bound for the Caribbean. On that first voyage, his ship was captured by pirates. Twelve-year-old Gustav did not think for very long about his fate. He willingly joined the attackers.

Before he was 20, Wilmerding was captain of his own pirate ship. And he was one of the most successful and feared pirates in the Caribbean.

Wilmerding's band was very important. He would not travel without a large number of musicians. For them, he had a special task.

Rather than just beating drums and blaring away at bugles, he ordered his musicians to ring bells. Wildly, they sent their melodies over the soft, tropical air. The effect was both noisy and disturbing to the enemy. Soon, the pirate became known as "Ding-Dong" Wilmerding.

After gathering a fortune in stolen treasures, he decided not to return to Europe. Once there, he could have been tried for his crimes and hanged.

Gathering some of his fellow pirate captains, he retired to the island of Little Thatch Cay, not far from Soper's Hole. There, he used his money to live like a rich man and enjoy an endless round of parties.

Some of Ding-Dong Wilmerding's descendants still live on nearby islands. And even today they share tales of ghostly sounds and flashing lights on Little Thatch Cay.

And perhaps, even today, they sometimes hear bells.

CHAPTER II

Captain William Kidd

WILLIAM Kidd was the most famous of all the pirates. He was born in Scotland in about 1645. His family was rich. Life was easy for young William.

As a young man, William went to sea for a time. Then he crossed the Atlantic to what is now New York. There he married. He and his wife, Sarah, had two daughters.

People knew William Kidd as an honest trader and sea captain. The most important citizens of New York were his friends. But, for some reason, Kidd wanted more adventure in his life.

The English and the French were once again fighting over land they both claimed in the New World. Here was something a man could be excited about. Kidd became a privateer for the English government.

The work was difficult because captains often raised the flag of another country over their ships to trick the privateers. By the time Kidd made sure he was chasing a French ship, it would be pulling away swiftly. Try as he might, he was not very successful at looting French ships.

Five years passed. Then, in 1695, King William III called Kidd back to England. An important Englishman, Lord Bellomont, had an offer to make. Bellomont and

King William III

Lord Bellomont

four of his friends wanted Kidd to be a pirate in search of pirates. It was Bellomont's task to get rid of piracy on the North American coast between New Jersey and Maine.

Now Kidd had two privateer assignments. The first was to attack French ships. The other was to find and board pirate vessels and arrest their captains.

He was given command of a 125-foot **schooner** called the *Adventure Galley*. It had 34 guns, 3 masts for its sails, and numerous holes for long oars called *sweeps*. When there was no wind, the ship could be rowed.

Captain Kidd and his crew of 150 left Plymouth, England, on April 23, 1696. The 284-ton *Adventure Galley* had not gone far when it was stopped by a British warship. The warship's forceful English captain came on board Kidd's ship and demanded 20 of his best seamen. Such a demand was not unusual during wartime. England's heavily armed warships were often short of crew.

Captain Kidd was furious. But the warship had many more men and better weapons. He could not fight back.

Without a full crew of 150, Kidd could not attack pirates. So he sailed for New York. The city was a gathering place for seamen, both honest and criminal. There, Kidd hired anyone he could. Finally, he had his new crew.

With this new crew, the *Adventure Galley* set out to find and attack pirates. But trouble came almost at once. Kidd's men did not think he was a strong leader. They wanted to rob every well-laden ship they met.

Kidd reminded his men over and over, "We have been commissioned to attack only the enemies of our king. He wants us to stop the other pirates. We may take their riches and their ships. But we are not to act the way they do."

The *Adventure Galley* came upon very few prize pirate ships. Some of those they found sailed swiftly away. This meant no pay for the crew.

A year passed. The men grew more and more angry with Captain Kidd.

One day, gunner William Moore lost his temper. He shouted at Kidd in front of the men. "You have ruined everything for us!" he cried.

Such shouting was a sign of great disrespect. Sea captains were supposed to be obeyed without question. Anything else was **mutiny**.

Kidd was furious. He grabbed a heavy wooden bucket held together by iron strips. Swinging it through the air, he aimed it at the seaman. It hit Moore in the head. The unfortunate gunner died the next day.

Aboard the ship, everyone was sullen and quiet. Kidd seemed unsure about what the men might do. By now they had gone almost two years without a raid to earn them money.

So the *Adventure Galley* became a true pirate ship. Its men began to attack any ship that might have riches of any kind.

Some historians say William Kidd was desperate and had listened to his crew's complaints. Others think the men took control of the ship away from him.

Soon other captains were calling Kidd "the pirate chaser who turned pirate."

The best prize Kidd's men captured was the *Quedagh Merchant*. It was a huge treasure ship of 400 tons. Its owners were Armenians. And the captain was English.

But when Kidd's men attacked, the *Quedagh Merchant* was flying a French flag. The wealth of this one vessel was so great that Captain Kidd's share alone was $60,000, a huge fortune in those days.

Rumors of Kidd's piracy began to reach England. The

One of the stories told about William Kidd was that he began his life as a pirate by burying his family's Bible.

government had changed. Pirates were no longer popular. Even the men who had paid for Kidd's trip would no longer support him. And now, there was a price on his head. He was even wanted for the gunner's murder.

Leaving the damaged *Adventure Galley*, Kidd took command of the *Quedagh Merchant* and sailed it to the island of Anguilla in the West Indies. There, he soon learned he was to be arrested in the first port he visited.

Kidd loaded his riches onto a **sloop**, the *San Antonio*. He hurried to set sail for New York. Off the New York shore, he anchored at Oyster Bay. His old friend, Lord Bellomont, was the new governor of the New York colony.

Certainly, he will protect me, Kidd thought.

42

But Captain Kidd had been gone for three years. And now he was an outlaw. Bellomont was not eager to help him.

Kidd was quickly arrested. He was weighed down by 16 pounds of chains and sent back to England.

Kidd spent the next two years in a filthy, crowded jail. Brought to trial, Captain William Kidd was sentenced to be hanged.

On the day of Kidd's execution, May 23, 1701, Londoners crowded the streets near where the Thames River meets the sea. Here, the famous Captain Kidd would be hanged.

Soon after the noose went around Kidd's neck, the rope broke. He fell into the mud below. The crowd roared with anger. After repairs were made, Kidd was again hanged. This time the rope held.

Captain Kidd's lifeless body was tied to a post near the sea. There, according to the custom of that day, it was washed by the tide three times. Then the body was forced into a wire cage. Men poured hot tar over it to keep it from rotting.

For many months, the body of William Kidd was left to hang at the mouth of the Thames River. At this spot, it could be seen by every sailor coming into London's port. It was a lesson to all who might want to become pirates.

Kidd's body hanging from the post

CHAPTER 12

Blackbeard the Pirate

BLACKBEARD was an English pirate whose real name was Edward Teach. He was a giant of a man. He stood six feet four inches tall and weighed 250 pounds. And he was ugly. In fact, it would be hard to imagine anyone more fierce-looking.

His huge, bushy beard covered his face from the eyes down. And his inky hair hung below his shoulders. He never smiled.

Some pirates liked to dress up in elegant clothes, but Blackbeard didn't. His favorite costume was a long, wide coat, stained and dribbled with food, liquor, and blood. Under it, he wore a rough shirt. It was open to the waist, showing a chest as hairy as an ape's. Below his belt were baggy breeches. Above, on his head of tangled hair, perched a battered felt hat.

Around his waist, Blackbeard wore a belt. From it hung a pair of cutlasses and a knife or two. With six pistols strapped to his chest, Blackbeard was dressed for the day.

But his fierce looks did not stop there. In order to appear even more frightening, Blackbeard braided **hemp** into his black hair and beard. Then he lit the strings of hemp. A frightening cloud of smoke rose around his head. If there was no time to braid the hemp, he simply stuck long, lighted matches under his hat.

Blackbeard's behavior was just as evil as his looks. And his soul was as black as his famous whiskers. He would raid any ship he came upon. And when things were dull, he sometimes robbed and killed his own men.

One of Blackbeard's favorite games was one he was good at himself. He would call his frightened crew together and then force them to go down into the ship's hold with him. There he **battened down** all the **hatches** so there was very little air. Then he lit several pots filled with sulfur. The men of the crew began to choke and cough. Blackbeard just laughed. The object was to see who could last the longest in the foul air. Of course, he himself always won. Then he would brag, "Can't you see? I'm the one who will live best in Hell!"

Strange as it may seem, Blackbeard was popular with the ladies. Dirty and mean as he was, he somehow managed to marry at least 14 young women! The last one was only 12 years old.

Not much is known about the later lives of these women, or whether he divorced each before marrying the next one. Some historians believe he murdered them all!

In his early days at sea, Blackbeard had sailed under the command of another pirate, Jack Hornigold. Afraid to keep such a nasty crewman, Hornigold was desperate to get Blackbeard off his ship. So he gave the younger man a ship of his own, the *Queen Anne's Revenge.*

Within a year, Blackbeard had captured enough other vessels to have his own fleet. Soon he was menacing all the shipping in the Bahama Islands.

In 1716, he sailed to the Carolina and Virginia coasts. He moved his base to Pamlico Sound. Along the way, he captured other ships, including one belonging to the pirate Stede Bonnet.

Once at Pamlico Sound, Blackbeard kept his ships hidden in rivers or behind sandbars. Then he attacked all the vessels that came his way.

Blackbeard had many tricks. Often he tried to decorate his ships so that other sailors would not recognize them. At least one time, he had his crew wear women's dresses and sunbonnets and carry parasols. When other captains came close, Blackbeard and his men fell upon them and seized their vessels.

Charleston Harbor

Because of these pirates, the planters of Virginia and the Carolinas could not safely send their goods across the Atlantic. And to make things worse, the governor of North Carolina protected Blackbeard from arrest in exchange for large money bribes.

In May of 1718, Blackbeard's ships blockaded Charleston Harbor for almost two weeks. The pirate demanded medicine for his crew. When it was delivered, the pirates robbed the men who brought it.

At last, the planters decided to take action. They pooled their money and persuaded the governor of Virginia to send ships to capture Blackbeard, dead or alive. The state of Virginia added a huge reward of 100 British pounds for Blackbeard's head.

One of the two Virginia ships was the H.M.S. *Pearl*. The man leading the search was Lieutenant Robert Maynard.

Before the English ships arrived at Pamlico Sound, Blackbeard shot off the kneecap of his first mate. "If I don't shoot somebody now and then," he roared in a drunken rage, "you'll forget who I am."

Before Blackbeard could sober up, Maynard's ships were sailing into Pamlico Sound, blocking the pirate's exit.

The first of Maynard's ships hit a sandbar. It was stuck tight. Blackbeard's pirates sailed in for the kill. But suddenly they found themselves **aground** too.

Maynard's second ship attacked. Blackbeard ordered his mighty cannons fired. When the smoke cleared, he could see only Maynard and one other Englishman on the deck of the *Pearl*. He ordered his pirates to board and loot the *Pearl*.

The attacking pirates climbed on deck. But they discovered they'd been tricked. From below rushed a crowd of slashing and shooting sailors. The pirates were hopelessly outnumbered. After a bloody battle, only Blackbeard was left alive.

Maynard and Blackbeard stood on deck, face to face. Each fired his pistol. Blackbeard's shot went wild. But Maynard's caught the pirate in the chest, just above his heart.

The shot had little effect! Snarling with rage, Blackbeard swung his cutlass. He broke Maynard's weapon in two. As the helpless lieutenant seemed about to die, his men rushed up.

Still the huge pirate fought on. With his throat cut and pistol shots peppering his body, he roared curses at his enemies. For a moment, he seemed stronger than death itself. Then slowly, like a slaughtered animal, he sank to the deck.

Maynard ordered Blackbeard's head cut off and hung from the **bowsprit** of the *Pearl*. The body of the pirate had more than 25 wounds. It was thrown overboard. There are those who say that, in the end, Blackbeard's headless body swam three times around the *Pearl* before it sank into the sea.

In 1996, remains of a ship were found in 24 feet of water off Beaufort, North Carolina. The vessel is believed to be the *Queen Anne's Revenge*. Cannons, barrel hoops, ballast stones, and a ship's bell have been raised to the surface. The search continues.

CHAPTER 13

Stede Bonnet, a Gentleman Pirate

WHEN Blackbeard was at his most powerful, he had a fleet of four pirate ships and 400 men. One of his captains was Major Stede Bonnet, a retired officer from the U.S. Army.

Bonnet did not always do things the same way as other pirates. He had no backers to buy him a vessel. And he was not a good enough seaman to steal someone else's ship.

Using his own money, he purchased and equipped a sloop, the *Revenge*. Then he armed it with ten guns and 70 men. Never before had a pirate paid for his own ship!

Bonnet loved to talk about his respected family and his good education. He had served honorably in the army. For a time, he had owned a farm on the Caribbean island of Barbados.

But it was the way he dressed that most drew attention to this clean-shaven, overweight captain. He wore a gentleman's powdered wig and fine clothes with plenty of gold braid. But his **dandy** ways and poor seamanship caused pirates like Blackbeard to laugh at him.

Finally, in the summer of 1718, Bonnet went off on his own. He plundered the Carolinas, Virginia, and Delaware.

Bonnet was captured after a battle off what is now South Carolina. He was taken to the city of Charleston. He escaped but was soon recaptured. After being tried for his crimes, Bonnet was executed in November 1718.

CHAPTER 14

Black Bart the Pirate

BARTHOLOMEW Roberts was a Welsh sailor who had been at sea for 20 years. Everyone around knew him as a hard worker and very knowledgeable seaman.

In 1719, his ship, the *Princess*, was captured by pirates led by Captain Howell Davis. Roberts was forced to board the pirate ship as a prisoner. He reluctantly agreed to become one of the pirate gang.

Six weeks later, Captain Davis was killed while attacking a Portuguese island. As the seaman with the most experience, Bartholomew Roberts was elected captain in his place.

Now happy in his role as pirate, Roberts allowed his strong personality to shine. He dressed in rich red waistcoats and breeches. A **tricorn** hat balanced on his head. A huge red feather protruded from it. A gold chain hung from his neck. From it dangled a diamond cross. A silk sling over his shoulder held two pairs of pistols. A sword swung at his side.

Roberts drank large quantities of tea. He believed that hard liquor made a crew less efficient.

It was the drinking of his crew that made Roberts a stern captain. He made all the men swear to obey his rules. For anyone who did not agree, he offered to fight a duel with swords or pistols.

One day, a crewman showed up very drunk and insulted Roberts in front of the other men. Roberts was furious and killed the man on the spot. When another sailor challenged him about this, the captain stabbed him with his sword. He then ordered the sailor whipped.

Roberts was now known as "Black Bart." For many months, he sailed the coast of Africa in his ship, *Royal Fortune.*

One morning, an English ship sent to search for pirates approached the *Royal Fortune*. Black Bart ran below. He hurriedly put on his red waistcoat, breeches, and his hat with the big red feather. He grabbed his sword and silk sling with the four pistols. Then he hung his gold chain around his neck.

Finally, the two ships came within range of each other. The English guns sent a fierce **broadside** toward the pirate ship. Black Bart's men fired back. When the smoke cleared, the men saw their captain slumped on the ropes of the deck. He had been killed by a shot through his neck.

Black Bart was 39 when he died. In four years, he had captured more than 400 ships. The entire Atlantic Ocean had been his hunting ground. Ships all along the coasts of North and South America and throughout the Caribbean had felt his fury.

Upon his death, his crew remembered his wishes. They threw his body overboard, still dressed in its red suit and hat. As the body began to sink, Black Bart's pistols and sword splashed into the water too.

A few hours later, the ship was captured. Black Bart's 169 seamen were held for trial. Most of them were put to death for their crimes.

The bodies of 18 of the men were dipped in tar, bound by metal straps, and hung from chains on three high hills along the African coast. It was a punishment similar to that of Captain Kidd in England 21 years before.

CHAPTER 15

Two Women Under the Jolly Roger Flag

THE Golden Age of Piracy on the east coast of North America lasted a little more than 30 years—from 1689 to 1720. Few people knew that sometimes women pirates were on board.

Young Anne Bonny was the child of a successful Irish lawyer, William Cormac. Her mother was Cormac's maid. To escape their shameful situation, Cormac took the maid and their baby across the sea to Charleston, South Carolina. There he became a wealthy merchant.

Anne was a stubborn girl with a quick temper. As she grew up, her parents wondered what would become of her. Clearly, she was not cut out for tending a home and garden.

While still in her teens, Anne married a poor, uneducated young man named James Bonny. He was a sailor and sometimes a pirate. Bonny took Anne to an island in the Bahamas.

Anne soon found out that the island's governor was paying her husband. Whenever pirates came ashore, James Bonny pointed them out. Then he testified against them.

Disgusted, Anne left him. For a time, she traveled with one pirate or another. But she never stayed long with any one of them.

Finally, she met the man of her dreams. He was pirate captain John Rackham. He was known throughout the Carolinas and northern Caribbean as "Calico Jack" because of his brightly colored clothes of many patterns. How Anne's heart raced as she watched him strut about a windswept deck!

Anne Bonny made her decision. She would give up petticoats and skirts. All she wanted was to marry Calico Jack and share his pirate adventures. She would even be willing to go into battle by his side.

Surprisingly, Calico Jack's crew of rowdies accepted Anne's presence on board. She cut her hair short and dressed in the baggy shirt and dungarees of a seaman. She could handle a rope, raise a sail, or wave a cutlass with the best of the crew.

"Calico Jack" Rackham

Soon Anne had a surprise. Not long after setting sail on Calico Jack's ship, she happened to meet a tall, thin sailor who had been on board only a few weeks. The newcomer shocked Anne by whispering an amazing truth. She, too, was a woman!

One night in a quiet corner of the deck, Mary Read told her story to Anne Bonny.

Mary was English by birth. She had lived with a grandmother who hated girls. The old woman dressed Mary as a boy from earliest childhood. And she treated the youngster like a favorite grandson.

When the grandmother died, Mary was frightened and alone. Could she suddenly switch to being a girl? Not feeling bold enough for this, she decided to continue her pose.

For a time, she served as cabin boy on a man-of-war. Later she was a foot soldier. Then she became a horseman in battles against the French army. Her record was so good that she was recommended for promotion as an officer. Somehow, she still kept secret the fact that she was a woman.

Her career changed, however, when she fell in love with a Dutch trooper. For the first time, she began to dress as a woman. The two were married. But Mary's happiness was short-lived. Her husband died a few months later.

Even as a widow, Mary was unwilling to give up adventuring. She cut her hair short again and went back to men's clothing. Then she boarded a Dutch ship headed for the West Indies.

On the way, the vessel was captured by pirates. Watching their daring actions, Mary knew what she wanted to do with the rest of her life. Piracy was now her dream. Once in the Indies, she signed on with Calico Jack Rackham. Finding his wife aboard as a pirate, Mary had decided to share her secret.

Only Anne Bonny and Calico Jack knew a second woman was on board. And things might have continued this way if romance had not come again to Mary Read.

One day, the pirates captured a merchant ship from Jamaica during a furious battle. One of the survivors of that ship was a handsome young carpenter. He was forced to join the crew of the pirate ship.

Mary fell hopelessly in love. Soon, she had whispered her secret to the startled young man. The couple planned to be married.

Anne Bonny (left) and Mary Read (right)

Mary's young carpenter was shy, mannerly, and small in size. Often he was teased and embarrassed by his rougher shipmates. One day, one of the burliest, most brutal members of the crew challenged the carpenter to a duel.

Mary was terrified for the safety of her lover. Still dressed as a man, she started a fight with that same burly crewman. She challenged him to a duel and set the time carefully. Mary would fight the man a few hours earlier than the time set for her husband-to-be's duel.

At dawn the next day, Mary and the bully met on the shore of a nearby island. With a single well-placed shot, Mary wounded the man. Then she ran him through with her cutlass. She had saved her carpenter from the threat of death. And through it all, the watching crew had no hint of her true identity.

One morning in 1720, bad luck came to Calico Jack and all aboard his ship. The crewmen were drunk and the guns not loaded. As almost everyone aboard dozed, the governor of Jamaica sent men out in a sloop to attack the pirate ship. They bore down on Calico Jack's vessel. Quickly, the governor's men scrambled aboard.

Only Anne Bonny and Mary Read were clearheaded enough to put up a fight. They slashed at the boarding party with their cutlasses. But they could not win such a battle by themselves. They had to surrender.

A month later, the pirate crew was on trial in Jamaica. Calico Jack broke Anne Bonny's heart. Trying to save himself, he swore that Anne and Mary were ruthless pirates. Then he called the two women the cruelest and most vicious of the entire crew.

As the trial came to an end, the judge ordered that all the pirates—both men and women—be put to death.

Hearing the sentence of the court, Anne and Mary stepped forward. They looked the judge boldly in the eye. "My Lord," they said together, putting their hands on their stomachs. "We plead our bellies!"

Both Anne Bonny and Mary Read were pregnant. Under the law, they could not be put to death. Soon the two women began prison sentences instead. They were to be executed after the birth of their babies.

Anne Bonny was allowed to visit Calico Jack the night before his death. She was still furious with him for not fighting to save his pirate ship. "Had you fought like a man," she told him, "you would not be hanged like a dog."

Mary Read died in prison before the birth of her baby. Her carpenter, having been forced into piracy, was set free.

There is no record of Anne Bonny's execution or of what happened to her baby. Some historians believe her wealthy father bought her freedom and took her home to South Carolina.

CHAPTER 16

Low and Phillips

A Terrible Reputation

ONE of the cruelest pirates in the Atlantic Ocean was English captain Edward Low. He often spared prisoners who were married men. But to those who had no family at home, he gave no quarter.

A story is told about one prisoner whose ears Low ordered cut off. Then the desperate man was forced to eat them with salt and pepper.

Low was captured off Long Island, New York, in 1723. He was then hanged for his crimes.

The Pickled Head of John Phillips

THE pirate John Phillips was killed in 1724 by his own crew. Many of the men had been forced into piracy by Phillips. They hated him!

The mutineers were led by another pirate, Captain Jonathan Haraden. Phillips had captured Haraden's fine, new ship and taken Haraden as prisoner. The angry prisoner **incited** the crew against Phillips.

The head of John Phillips was later delivered to Boston. It had been pickled in a tub of salty brine.

CHAPTER 17

Privateers and the American Revolution

WHEN the American Revolution began in 1776, America's small Continental navy was forced to face the huge British navy. America's navy had only 34 vessels.

As many European nations had done, the colonists fought with the help of privateers. Ships were built in ports such as Plymouth, Massachusetts, and Baltimore, Maryland. These swift ships attacked the British and blocked ports on the east coast from attack.

America's success in the Revolutionary War depended, in part, upon these attacks from the sea.

CHAPTER 18

Jean Lafitte

THE last of the Atlantic pirates was a tall, slim, fair-skinned Frenchman named Jean Lafitte(la-FEET). He ruled the swamps of Barataria Bay near New Orleans. Pierre Lafitte joined his brother for a while. They commanded 1,000 pirates. Their raiding parties controlled the Mississippi Delta and a good deal of the Gulf of Mexico.

The Lafittes were pirates, not privateers. Working only for themselves, Jean and his brother ordered attacks against the ships of any nation. Cruelly, they killed all crew members of captured ships so there would be no witnesses.

The authorities in Louisiana in 1809 were anxious to stop these wild pirate raids. The United States had purchased Louisiana from France only six years earlier. New settlers were needed there. No one wanted them frightened away by pirates.

Jean Lafitte

Governor Claiborne

For many months, Governor Claiborne of Louisiana searched for an answer. In 1810, he formed a coast guard of 40 men to sail against the pirates.

Jean Lafitte looked out to sea with his large, dark eyes. He saw the governor's 40 men and their few, small ships. These were no threat to him! If they came close, he would deal with them easily.

But Lafitte soon found himself in a different kind of trouble.

He had sunk an American ship, the *Independence*. As he smuggled the stolen goods into New Orleans to sell them, he had a rude surprise. He was arrested.

The captain of the *Independence* had hidden under a sail when the pirates raided his ship. He stayed hidden as they set fire to the vessel. As it sank, this one survivor grabbed a piece of wreckage. He floated low in the water so no one would see him.

After Lafitte and his men sailed away, the captain swam toward land. Before long, he was picked up by a passing ship. He made his way back to New Orleans. Now he was ready to testify against Jean Lafitte.

But the pirate would not give up easily. The day after his arrest, Lafitte broke out of the jail. He escaped back to Barataria Bay.

The governor was furious. He offered $500 for the capture of Lafitte. The reward was a huge sum of money at that time.

The pirate answered with an offer of his own. He would pay $1,500 for the capture of the governor!

But soon Governor Claiborne's attention turned away from Lafitte and his band of pirates. The War of 1812 had begun. American troops were needed to fight the British. No men could be spared to hunt down pirates in the swamps of Barataria Bay.

On September 2, 1814, a strange thing happened. The British government made Lafitte an offer. They wanted help in attacking the Americans in New Orleans. If Lafitte would join the British, they would give him $30,000. And they would make him a captain in the British army. They would even pardon all his pirates for their crimes!

But Lafitte was like many Frenchmen at that time. He hated the English. He kept them waiting for his answer.

In the meantime, Lafitte sent a message to Governor Claiborne. He warned of the British attack. And he made a surprising offer. He and his men would help defend New Orleans.

The governor refused. He hated Lafitte as much as he hated the English enemy. So he answered by having six ships fire their cannons at Lafitte's men at Barataria Bay. The pirates escaped into the swamps.

The city of New Orleans waited for the English attack. Its 1,000 men had little ammunition. Some had no weapons at all. And the British force was made up of 12,000 experienced soldiers. The people of New Orleans were terrified.

General Andrew Jackson

President James Madison sent General Andrew Jackson to New Orleans with orders to defend the city. One of the first things Jackson did was go looking for Jean Lafitte. Would the pirates be willing to fight with Jackson's men?

Lafitte smiled. At last, someone realized how much he loved his adopted country. Of course, he would fight for her!

In a fierce battle on December 23, 1814, the Americans and the pirates fought side by side at a Louisiana plantation. Quickly, a fog rolled in.

A group of Americans came creeping through the tall grass. They were riflemen from Tennessee. And they were excellent marksmen. With them came the pirates with their swords. One by one, they found and killed the British soldiers in the heavy mist.

The British enemy lost 700 men. The Americans and Lafitte lost only 31.

On January 8, 1815, the British attacked the city once more. Again the pirates fought bravely with Jackson's men.

This time, the British lost 2,600 troops. Only 13 Americans were killed. New Orleans was saved!

For a time, Lafitte was well respected. But not for long. He would not give up his pirate ways.

In 1817, he sailed to Galveston Island off the coast of Texas. There he started a new pirate city. Once again he became powerful.

In 1821, the pirates raided the Louisiana coast and sank an American ship. The U.S. government answered by sending troops to destroy the pirate colony at Galveston. Not wanting to fight Americans, Lafitte gave in. He set fire to his own town, sailed away, and disappeared. Most historians believe he lived quietly for five more years, probably on the Yucatan Peninsula of Mexico.

CHAPTER 19

California's Pirate

IN the late 1600s, pirates and privateers grew rich attacking the ships of the **Spanish Main**. But no one cared about other Spanish properties that included stretches of desert land along the coast of the Pacific Ocean.

Small, poor tribes of natives and a few Russian fishermen lived there. Indeed, before the discovery of gold in 1848, few could imagine any treasures coming out of what would later be called California.

We know that Sir Francis Drake had stopped in 1579. He had left a plaque at New Albion, which was north of what is now San Francisco. He had claimed the land for England. But the English government was unable to govern a land so far away. So a settlement at New Albion was never formed.

It was almost 250 years later that a Frenchman, Hippolyte de Bouchard, came to North America's Pacific coast. His purpose was not to find new land. And he did not expect to steal many riches. His was a different plan.

As a young man, Bouchard had moved from France to Buenos Aires, Argentina. There he married a woman from a wealthy family and settled down. He had been well schooled in French. But he had also learned Spanish and English.

Argentina, at that time, was under the rule of Spain.

In 1816, after six years of struggle, the provinces of Argentina declared their independence from Spain. The people of the new nation were proud. One of the proudest citizens was Hippolyte de Bouchard. "What is wrong with the other Spanish colonies?" he asked his friends. "Why don't they fight against the wicked Spanish Crown too?"

Impatient, Bouchard formed a plan. He would sail around the tip of South America and work his way up to California. Once there, he would insist that the Spanish province of Alta California break away from the mother country.

Bouchard's ship, *La Argentina,* reached the Pacific Ocean early in 1818. Instead of landing in California, he sailed

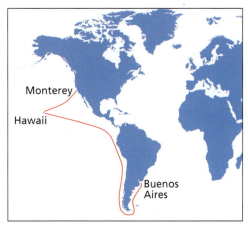

west to the Sandwich Islands, now called Hawaii. There he loaded supplies onto his vessel and bought another ship, the *Santa Rosa,* from Hawaiian King Kamehameha. The smaller ship's English captain, Peter Corney, agreed to sail with Bouchard.

King Kamehameha

The crews of the two ships were a strange combination of men. There were seamen of all nations. Many of them were cutthroats and thieves. Some had jumped ship in the islands. Others were hiding from the law. Last to be brought on board were 250 *kanakas,* or natives of the islands. Used to warm, tropical weather, they dressed in very little clothing and knew nothing of dealing with the cold.

Bouchard sailed east from Hawaii with his two ships. "I will teach those Californios a lesson," he told his officers. "Since they

will not rise up against the Spanish government, I will punish them."

He turned the bows of his two pirate ships toward the port city of Monterey. It was the capital of Alta California.

On September 21, 1818, the two ships sailed into Monterey Bay. The *Santa Rosa* led. Hoping luck was on their side, the pirates opened fire. But a horseman had ridden into Monterey to give warning.

To Bouchard's surprise, a troop of defenders on shore protected Monterey's *presidio,* or fort. The soldiers let loose with large bursts from their cannons. The *Santa Rosa* suffered a direct hit. Her mast was cut nearly in two.

But this was just a lucky shot. The soldiers had very little gunpowder. And their cannons were rusty.

The people of Monterey had fled the town. They left only a small group to defend the city. Loading carts and mounting horses, they rushed to the ranches and missions inland. Only a few soldiers remained on the beach.

Meanwhile, Bouchard sent 200 men and several large guns ashore at a cove called Point Piños. His forces quickly lined up and began to march along the shore toward town, five miles away.

The pirates arrived to find Monterey nearly deserted. Quickly, they entered the fort and set it ablaze. Then the pirates stole all they could find of value from the homes. They tore up gardens and destroyed orchards. Finally, they raised the Argentine flag over the town.

As the pirates loaded furniture, clothes, and food onto their ships, a work crew began repairs on the *Santa Rosa.*

Three days later, the repairs were finished. The pirates raised anchor on their two ships and sailed south along the coast.

Near what is now Santa Barbara, California, the pirates attacked the ranch of a prosperous Spaniard and burned the buildings. Again, they claimed the land for Argentina.

Still farther south, the pirates came to a fine harbor. Leaving their ships, they marched inland to attack the mission at nearby San Juan Capistrano.

But the padres at the mission had been warned by horseback riders hurrying south. The mission's gold altar decorations and fine robes had already been carefully hidden. There was little of value to steal.

When the pirates burst into the mission's courtyard, they found the padres hurrying to pour the church's sacred wine onto the ground.

The infuriated seamen pushed the priests aside and began to drink what had not yet been wasted. There was no one to fight here and little to steal.

When the wine was gone, the pirates were very drunk. Some who had passed out had to be tied to cannons and rolled back to the ships.

Not happy with the result of their raid at San Juan Capistrano, the hapless pirates lifted their anchors and sailed south. They were not seen again. Certainly, the people of California were glad to be rid of them.

The Argentine government never followed up on the settlements claimed by Bouchard. And his attacks did not succeed in causing Californios to rise up against Spain as he had planned.

CHAPTER

Piracy Comes to an End in the New World

As trade increased in the late 1800s, the nations of the Americas grew richer. Now they could afford the protection of better navies.

Governments in the new territories became more honest. Merchant ships were better armed. And there was greater cooperation between nations to make sure laws were obeyed.

For all of these reasons, piracy began to disappear. Today, we find most stories of robbery on the high seas in books like *Treasure Island* or in action films from movie and television studios.

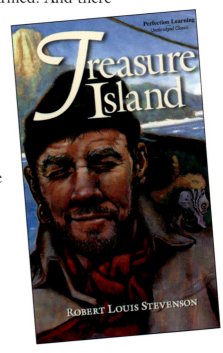

Glossary

aft — referring to the rear part of a ship

aground — stuck on or sailed onto the shore

batten down — to close and make secure

blockade — to use warships or troops to stop traffic in or out of an area

bow — referring to the forward part of a ship

bowsprit — large pole extending forward on a ship

bribery — act of exchanging money or goods for a favor

broadside — gunfire from several weapons along one side of a ship at once

buccaneer — raider of Spanish ships and settlements in the West Indies in the 17th century

caravel — small, light ship; faster than a nao (see separate glossary entry)

careen — to turn a ship on its side to clean and repair it

commission — to grant the power to perform certain acts or duties

corsair — type of pirate ship used along the Barbary Coast of North Africa

Crown — government ruled by a king or queen

cutlass — short, curved, thick sword better suited for the slashing fights aboard ships than long swords

dandy — paying unusual attention to personal appearance

execution — act or process of putting to death

forecastle — forward part of the upper deck of a ship

galleon	large sailing ship having three or more masts (see separate glossary entry)
galley	low, flat vessel, propelled partly or wholly by oars
hatch	covered opening in a ship's deck
hemp	fiber from a plant in the mulberry family used to make rope
hold	cargo deck of a ship, usually below the top deck
hornpipe	lively folk dance of the British Isles
hull	frame or body of a ship
incite	to move to action
indentured servant	person who signs and is bound by a contract to work for another for a specified time in return for payment of travel and living expenses
jig	any of several lively springy dances in triple rhythm
keel	part of a ship that extends along the bottom from the front to the back
lanteen sail	triangular sail
loot	valuables taken by force or violence
man-of-war	combat ship of a navy
maritime	relating to navigation or commerce on the sea
maroon	to put ashore and abandon a person on a barren island
mast	long pole that rises from the deck of a ship that holds the rigging and sails
merchant seaman	person working on a ship for a company
mutiny	revolt against discipline or a superior officer
nao	means "ship" in Spanish. Today, we call such a ship a *carrack*. It was a fat, slow ship, designed for hauling cargo.

patach	small, easy-to-maneuver ship
piece of eight	piece of an old Spanish coin
pirate	person who commits robbery on the high seas
plight	unfortunate, difficult, or dangerous situation
plunder	to take something by force
privateer	pirate (see separate glossary entry) working for a particular government; attacks ships of another government
quarter	mercy shown to a defeated opponent
ruffian	brutal person
rum	alcoholic beverage made from fermented sugarcane
sack	to take valuables from a captured town
schooner	two-masted ship
sea chantey	song sung by sailors in rhythm with their work
sea dog	veteran sailor
sloop	single-masted ship rigged front and back with a long bowsprit (see separate glossary entry); favored by many pirates because it was easy to maneuver
Spanish Armada	fleet of armed ships that tried to invade England in 1588; thought to be undefeated
Spanish Main	mainland of Spanish America, from the Isthmus of Panama to the present republics of Colombia and Venezuela
square-rigged	having the main sails extended on a pole fastened to the masts (see separate glossary entry) horizontally and at the center
stern	back part of a ship
tricorn	having three corners

Index

Africa, 24, 25, 51
Alta California, 64, 65
American Revolution, 5, 58
Argentina, 64, 66
Atlantic Ocean, 6, 12, 14, 16, 24, 39, 47, 51, 57
Bahama Islands, 46, 52
Barataria Bay, 59, 60, 61
Barbados, 49
Bazán, Don Alvaro de, 15–16
Bellomont, Lord, 5, 39–40, 42–43
Bonnet, Stede, 5, 46, 49
Bonny, Anne, 5, 52–56
Bonny, James, 52
Bouchard, Hippolyte de, 5, 63–66
California, 5, 25, 63, 64, 66
Cape of Good Hope, 25
Carib Indians, 31
Caribbean Sea, 4, 8, 11, 20, 24, 34, 36, 37, 38, 49, 51, 52
Cartagena, Venezuela, 31
Charles II, 36
Charleston, South Carolina, 5, 47, 49, 52
Chile, 33
Claiborne, Governor, 60, 61
Cormac, William, 52
Corney, Peter, 64
Cortés, Hernando, 14
Cuba, 29, 30
Davis, Captain Howell, 50
Drake, Sir Francis "The Dragon," 4, 23–26, 63
Elizabeth I, 23, 26
England, 4, 5, 17, 23, 24, 25, 26, 36, 39, 40, 42, 43, 51, 63, 70
France, 27, 28, 59, 64
Galveston Island, 62

Gibraltar, Venezuela, 31, 34, 35
Haraden, Captain Jonathan, 57
Hawkins, John, 4, 23–24, 26
Hispaniola, 11, 24
Hornigold, Jack, 46
Jackson, Andrew, 61, 62
Jamaica, 34, 35, 36, 54, 55
Kidd, William "Captain," 5, 39–43, 51
King Kamehameha, 64
Lafitte, Jean, 5, 59–62
Lafitte, Pierre, 59
Lake Maracaibo, 34, 35
Las Perlas Island, 31
Little Thatch Cay, 38
Low, Edward, 5, 57
Madison, James, 61
Magellan, Ferdinand, 26
Maracaibo, Venezuela, 31, 34, 35
Maynard, Robert, 47–48
Mexico, 6, 14, 25, 62
Modyford, Governor, 34
Moore, William, 41
Morgan, Henry "Morgan the Terrible," 4, 32–36
Nau, Jean-David "L'Olonnois the Cruel," 4, 27–31
New Albion, 25, 63
New Orleans, Louisiana, 5, 59, 60, 61, 62
New York, 39, 40, 42, 57
Pacific Ocean, 25, 63, 64
Pamlico Sound, North Carolina, 46, 47
Panama, 4, 23, 24, 33, 36, 70
Peru, 6, 14, 23
Phillips, John, 5, 57
Pizarro, Francisco, 14

Porto Bello, Panama, 33–34
Puerto Cabello, Venezuela, 31
Puerto Principe, Cuba, 32
Rackham, "Calico Jack," 5, 52, 53, 54, 55, 56
Read, Mary, 5, 53–56
Roberts, Bartholomew "Black Bart," 5, 50–51
San Juan Capistrano, 66
ships
  Adventure Galley, 40, 41, 42
  caravel, 12, 14, 68
  corsair, 28, 68
  galleon, 6, 7, 8, 16, 17, 18, 33, 69
  galley, 15, 69
  Golden Hind, 25
  Independence, 60
  Judith, 23, 24
  La Argentina, 64
  Magdalena, 35, 36
  man-of-war, 7, 30, 53, 69
  nao, 13, 14, 68, 69
  patach, 16, 70

Pearl, 47, 48
Princess, 50
Quedagh Merchant, 41, 42
Queen Anne's Revenge, 46, 48
Revenge, 49
Royal Fortune, 51
San Antonio, 42
Santa Rosa, 64, 65
schooner, 40, 70
sloop, 42, 49, 55, 70
Seville, Spain, 12, 14, 24
Soper's Hole, 38
Spanish Armada, 4, 26, 70
St. Augustine, Florida, 16
Strait of Magellan, 25
Teach, Edward "Blackbeard," 5, 44–48, 49
Thames River, 43
War of 1812, 5, 61
West Indies, 27, 42, 54
William III, 39
Wilmerding, Gustav "Ding-Dong," 4, 38